I0465405

THIS BOOK

BELONGS TO

....

....

I can't tell you how grateful I am that you decided to read my book. My most heartfelt thanks that you took time out of your life to choose my work and I hope you find benefit within these pages.

There are so many books available today that offer similar content so that makes it even more humbling that you decided to buying mine.

Tell me what you thought! I am eager to hear your opinion and ideas on what you read as are others who are looking for a good book to buy. Leave a review on Amazon.com so others can benefit from your wisdom!

With much thanks.

@COPYRIGHT 2024

The content contained within this book may not be reproduced, duplicated, or transmitted without direct written permission from the author or the publisher. Under no circumstances will any blame or legal responsibility be held against the publisher, or author, for any damages, reparation, or monetary loss due to the information contained within this book. Either directly or indirectly.

Legal Notice:
This book is copyright protected. This book is only for personal use. You cannot amend, distribute, sell, use, quote, or paraphrase any part, or the content within this book, without the consent of the author or publisher.

Disclaimer Notice:
Please note the information contained within this document is for educational and entertainment purposes only. All effort has been executed to present accurate, up-to-date, and reliable, complete information. No warranties of any kind are declared or implied. Readers acknowledge that the author is not engaging in the rendering of legal, financial, medical, or professional advice. The content within this book has been derived from various sources. Please consult a licensed professional before attempting any techniques outlined in this book. By reading this document, the reader agrees that under no circumstances is the author responsible for any losses, direct or indirect, which are incurred as a result of the use of the information contained within this document, including, but not limited to — errors, omissions, or inaccuracies.

Table of Contents

Introduction

We can understand data mining better if we split it into two words: Data and Mining. Understanding these two words individually will lay the foundation to understand Data Mining as a whole.

Information that is formatted and structured in a particular way is known as data. Today, we associate the term data with the domain of computing, mostly. The term program also draws parallels to the term data today. Data processed through a set of instructions are called programs. Data is available in all forms such as images, text, numbers, and can be stored on a piece of paper and digital media. However, in the 21st century, data mostly refers to information stored and transmitted through digital mediums.

When we talk about mining in general, it refers to the extraction of materials that are present deep inside the earth. Examples of mining are coal mining, gold mining, diamond mining, etc.

If we now merge both these terms, Data Mining in the field of computer science is the extraction of information from raw data sources that can be used for the benefit of a business or otherwise. Do not compare the term data mining to the general mining process as it can confuse you. When miners extract gold or diamonds from the surface of the earth, the result is gold and diamonds. However, the result of data mining is not data. The objective behind data mining is to extract information from raw data to recognize patterns that will give us insights about the respective data set belonging to a particular domain in life. This is why data mining is often referred to as Knowledge Extraction or Knowledge Discovery.

Gregory Piatetsky-Shapiro became the first person to associate the phrase Knowledge Discovery with Data Mining in 1989. As the years passed, the term Data Mining gained popularity. Today, however, the terms data mining and knowledge discovery are interchangeable.

If there is a process today where the requirement is to deal with huge sets of data, the first approach towards it is data mining. For example, Netflix will look at all the data they have on movies that you have already watched and will use it to suggest movies as per your liking to you. Websites like Amazon will look at your purchase and spend patterns and target you with similar products in the price range you're comfortable with.

Chapter One: Overview of Data Mining

Purpose of Data Mining

Raw data can be very confusing and almost useless. However, when information is extracted from raw data and organized and structured properly, it can reveal patterns and information that would otherwise be hidden. When a business can understand the historic patterns of a data set, it can leverage this information to predict future trends and behavior. Ultimately, this helps a business to improve its decision-making process.

Technically, data mining uses computing power to analyze data from all available sources, angles, perspectives, and dimensions and further classifying it such that it makes sense. Data mining has multiple applications such as data warehousing, transactional databases, relational databases, multimedia databases, and even the World Wide Web.

In short, data mining helps to classify data such that businesses can learn about the various trends and patterns in a data set to benefit the business. There are countless benefits of data mining. Some of them are risk management, fraud detection, spam mail filtering, marketing, etc. It can further be leveraged even to understand the sentiments of end customers.

Steps Involved in Data Mining

Let us quickly go through the various steps that are part of the data mining process.

1. The first step is to extract raw data, convert it, and store it in a data warehouse.
2. Data is transferred from the data warehouse to various databases so that it can be managed efficiently.

3. Provide access to the data to business analysts via dashboards.
4. Use data visualization techniques to represent huge data sets so that senior leaders and stakeholders of a business can understand data in one glance.

Let us go through the four steps mentioned above in detail.

Data Extraction

The first step is to extract data and store it as per the requirement of the respective business. Data can be of different types. It can be transactional for any business or it may just be metadata or non-operational data. Data is referred to as metadata when its design is in the form of a logical database. In contrast, non-operational data is data that is usually forecasted.

A business can improve its revenue significantly by understanding patterns in data as it holds critical and useful information. Customer-focused businesses deal with huge amounts of data and data mining can help them understand their customers better. It gives them an elaborate picture of the spending patterns and purchase-power of their customers. It also helps them compare their products and pricing with rival firms.

For example, Walmart is one of the biggest retail giants globally and has tons of data on their customers and how they interact with the organization. Walmart leverages data mining to understand the patterns of its customers and in turn, uses it to improve its revenue. This data is also disclosed to various vendors of Walmart so that they can understand customer behavior too. The data of concern to such retail organizations include days when sales are at their peak, holiday sales, most shopped products, and other relevant data.

Design and Develop Data Mining Models

The second step mentioned above deals with designing and developing data mining models. In this step, a business decides what kind of algorithm suits their requirements and can mine data efficiently. Algorithms help you to recognize patterns in a data set and provide outputs to help a business further. Algorithms such as regression and classification algorithms can provide the relationship between elements in a data set to empower the business. Since data mining has gained a lot of popularity over the years, there are predefined algorithms developed by Oracle and SQL today that can be used in a data mining model. Some of these algorithms are used for regression and clustering to give a structure to the data available.

Accessibility

Now that the data is structured and classified, the next step is to make it accessible to the business. A business has multiple teams working to make it successful. The extracted data can be made accessible to various teams such as marketing, sales, etc. They can use it to plan their strategies better. Marketing teams can use the data to understand where to invest marketing funds such that the return on investment is optimum. Sales teams can use this data to target customers at the right time with the right set of products.

Visualization

Finally, the data needs to be plotted visually using charts so that even teams and individuals who have not worked deeply on the data understand it in one glance. Senior leaders of a team do not have the time to go through heaps of data stored in tables and sheets. Therefore, presenting the data to them in a visual form such that they understand the current state of the business will help them make decisions for the future.

Uses of Data Mining

Let us look at the common areas where businesses use data mining daily.

Market Management and Analysis using Data Mining

Data mining has proved to be very effective for market management and analysis purposes. Data mining can be applied successfully to the following market areas.

Customer Profiling

Data mining can be used by a business to understand the nature of their customers. Insights can reveal the kind of spending power customers have and the products they purchase.

Customer Requirements

Businesses can employ data mining to know which products best suit the requirements of their customers. Data mining techniques can be employed to sell existing products to new customers or sell new products to existing customers.

Cross Market Analysis

Data mining can be used to understand the association between different product sales. This information can be used to upsell a new product to an existing customer along with their regular product.

Targeting Specific Markets

Data Mining can be used to create cluster models so that customers in a specific group with similar tastes and habits can be targeted with a common product.

Purchase Patterns

Data mining can help businesses to identify the purchase patterns of various customers. This information can be used to sell more products to customers that have similar purchase patterns.

Reports

Data mining provides a summary of data in a multidimensional format.

Risk Management and Analysis

Businesses employ data mining in the following areas that help with risk management and analysis.

Financial Planning and Analysis

Data mining is used by organizations for financial planning and analysis of the cash inflow and evaluating their assets.

Resource Planning

Data mining helps to analyze and plan the resources against the expenditure for an organization.

Competition from Rivals

Data mining can be used by a business to gain knowledge about their rivals and learn the direction of the market.

Fraud Detection

Technology has helped make life easy for the common man but it has also resulted in online frauds becoming a common occurrence. Millions of people enter their credit card information on the Internet daily. Data mining can be employed to register fraudulent activities concerning credit cards and telecommunication based on the irregularities in the spending patterns. Therefore, data mining can help prevent fraud before it takes place. Data mining can help register information such as the name of the caller, the recipient of the call, the timestamp, the duration of the call, etc. For credit cards, information such as the IP address, the browser, the operating system used, timestamp, etc. can be registered using data mining.

Chapter Two: Data Mining and Data Science

Data Mining and Data Science run in parallel with each other. In this chapter, we will take you through the techniques that are important for you to become a data mining or data science professional. We will also draw parallels between data mining and data science in this chapter to understand the similarities and the differences between the two.

We already know that data is increasing exponentially in the world every day and that data is the new currency. Data is a very important aspect of growing organizations. But just data is not sufficient. The huge amount of data gives rise to the need for tools to sort and analyze the data that organizations collect to boost their revenue. This also gives rise to the profile of data analysts and data scientists as there is a lot of data that needs to be sorted and organized since raw data has information that is significant to organizations to make better decisions. Businesses make use of various analytics techniques to gain insights from the data that they have collected.

The requirement for data analysis has given birth to 4 important data analytics techniques that are as follows.

- Descriptive analytics
- Prescriptive analytics
- Diagnostic analytics
- Predictive analytics

Let us go through each of these techniques one by one to understand them and know where they are used.

Descriptive Analysis

As suggested by the name, the process of descriptive analysis takes all the raw data collected from various sources. It converts it into a descriptive format to make it easier for humans to understand the data. This means that historic patterns of data are described elaborately using this analytics approach. A business can use descriptive analysis to learn past patterns of customers to predict their future behavior. This helps businesses to be prepared with strategies for an event even before the event takes place. Descriptive analytics is the most common approach to analytics employed by most organizations. Descriptive analytics help to create future measures and key metrics for any kind of business model.

Prescriptive Analysis

The process of breaking down raw data step by step for a given scenario is known as prescriptive analysis. Let us go through an example to understand this better. Consider that you want to go out and you have booked an Uber. The Uber driver needs to come to your house to pick you up, but the regular route to your house has more than usual traffic that day. In a situation like this, Google maps will instantly suggest an alternate route. This is precisely where prescriptive analysis comes into the picture. The Google maps algorithm analyzed the current situation and quickly identified that the regular route has traffic that may result in poor customer experience. Therefore, based on the situation, it quickly checked for alternate routes so that the Uber driver could reach you as soon as possible. It ensured that no time was wasted despite traffic leading to better customer experience.

Diagnostic Analytics

Diagnostic analytics is the successor of descriptive analytics. The root cause of a problem can be reached with the help of diagnostic analytics as it helps data analysts and data scientists to deep dive into data. The tools available to businesses for diagnostic analytics and descriptive analytics work in tandem with each other.

Predictive Analytics

Foresight and vision are key aspects of a successful business. Predictive analytics helps achieve this. Predictive analytics basically analyzes present-day data to forecast future trends and patterns. Predictive analytics and be scarily accurate at times. It can predict whether an event will occur or not in the future and sometimes may even predict the exact timestamp for the event occurring in the future. Predictive analytics picks up co-dependent variables in a data set to learn what is exactly trending. Let us look at healthcare as an example. Data for the current lifestyle of an individual can be studied to predict how they will be at the age of forty. Several variables affect this analysis such as diet, exercise, traveling, city life, etc. By studying these variables, a doctor may even predict the diseases an individual is likely to contract in the future. It can be concluded that predictive analytics can be employed across all fields of life.

Techniques Needed for Aspiring Data Analytics or Data Science Professionals

Different businesses have different requirements when it comes to the data they need. Therefore, there are various kinds of analysis techniques that they use to retrieve and extract data. The end result of what is done with the extracted data depends on the domain that the business operates in. Businesses employ multiple techniques for data analysis and data science that offer different types of insights to them. Since the end result is not known to the data analyst or data scientist, it can often get confusing for both while generating and classifying the data. But you do not need to worry, as the essential thing to do here is to know what part of your data is relevant to the business requirements and this can be easily figured out by understanding patterns in the data set.

Let us discuss the most common techniques used by organizations in the data mining activity.

Anomaly Detection

When you are mining data, you will go through huge data sets with patterns hidden in them as expected, but now and then you will come across instances of data that do not belong in that data set. This odd instance of data is known as an anomaly and the process of finding anomalies in a data set is known as anomaly detection. Other synonyms are used for anomalies such as outliers, exceptions, contaminants, surprises, etc. An anomaly is not always a bad thing to have in a data set. Their presence can help derive valuable insights too. Outliers can be described as instances of data that deviate from the general standard of data in the data set or deviate from the pattern that the data set is generating as a whole. For instance, if our data set had numbers in the range of 5 to 7, the number 11 in the data set would be an outlier. This would mean that there is something odd about this instance and should be investigated further to see if it reveals unexpected information.

Anomaly detection leads to curiosity in data scientists and data analysts too as they then thrive on knowing if this irregularity was caused due to risk or fraud. They would then do a deeper analysis of the data and pass the information to the security team so that if there are loopholes in the system, they can be patched. Therefore, anomaly detection is a critical process that lets a business know if their system is flawed. It also helps a business to understand the reasons why certain aspects of the business strategy may be failing.

Data analysts and scientists should be okay with the fact that small sets of anomalies will always come up when they are dealing with huge sets of data, especially during the process of data mining. Usually, anomalies are a deviation from the regular pattern of the data set but there are times when they can be completely random. They can be very interesting concerning statistics as well.

Clustering Analysis

Clustering analysis refers to identifying groups of data in a data set that exhibit similar attributes. The analysis is used to understand the similarities and differences between groups of data in a data set. Clustering leads to the discovery of common traits in data, which can be used to create better algorithms to empower precise targeting. For instance, consider a data set that shows the purchasing patterns of customers. Using this information, a retail business can analyze the purchasing power of various customers or groups of customers to target them with more products that fall in the same range, in turn boosting the revenue.

Clustering analysis also results in personal development. What this means is a business will create fictional characters and classify customers as a particular character based on the attributes of that character. The attributes will include age group, purchasing power, regular products, salary range, etc. Customers with these attributes will be assigned the fictional character they fit and the business will then target the products assigned to these characters to the customers.

Association Analysis

Businesses use association analysis to understand the relevant association between data sets and their variables in a huge database. Association analysis can help you to reveal hidden data in data sets that are otherwise difficult to find. It helps to locate covert instances of data in a data set and also tells us if these covert instances of data are recurring in the data set.

Association analysis is very helpful from a sales point of view as it helps to find hidden patterns that can help make unusual sales that bring in huge revenue. Businesses can recommend new products to customers based on their purchase history using association analysis. Additionally, new products can be suggested to customers to be bundled with their regular purchases for the month. Association analysis, if used efficiently, can boost sales for a retail business and improve the conversion rates significantly.

Let us look at an example to understand association analysis. Walmart used data mining techniques in 2005 to analyze historical data of their customers. They learned that whenever there was a weather forecast for a hurricane, the sales of strawberry pops would increase seven times the regular sales. Walmart capitalized on this opportunity by placing strawberry pops at the checkout counters so that everyone would stock them up when there was a forecast of a hurricane. The placement at the checkout counter ensured that customers who would usually not buy strawberry pops also bought it.

Regression Analysis

Attributes of data in a data set are mostly co-dependent. Therefore it is beneficial if we can learn about their dependencies. Regression analysis comes into the picture when you want to learn about dependencies of attributes on each other. We assume that an attribute has a single-way effect on another attribute's response in a data set.

Even when attributes are independent of each other, they are still influenced in one way or the other by the presence of other attributes in the data set. However, this does not indicate any mutual dependency between the attributes. Therefore you can use regression analysis to learn that one variable in a data set is dependent on another variable but the vice-versa does not hold

Regression analysis is also used to understand customer satisfaction and how attributes affect customer loyalty. It also helps businesses to understand if attributes affect service levels as well.

Lately, regression analysis has also proved to be efficient for dating applications and websites by providing satisfactory results to the users of dating applications. Dating applications employ regression analysis to understand the likes and dislikes of users to match them based on their attributes producing better results.

Data mining and data science have made things very comfortable for businesses today by focusing only on relevant information. This ultimately results in creating business models that help businesses predict customer patterns and behavior leading to better conversation rates.

The collection of information always helps to build better business models. Business models can be used to employ data mining processes to information that in turn helps in gradually increasing the revenue of a business.

Classification Analysis

The systematic approach of gathering crucial and relevant information about data in a data set is known as classification analysis. Businesses deal with a lot of data daily and not all of it is important. Classification analysis helps categorize data into one that is important and useful to the business. Classification analysis and clustering analysis go hand in hand as classification of data is a prerequisite to the clustering of data. The biggest application of classification analysis is Email Hosting. Email hosting providers make use of classification algorithms to categorize an email to be either legit or spam. This is done using the metadata that is available in the headers of an incoming email. There are parameters such as from and to address, subject, origin IP, etc. in the headers of an email. Classification analysis may also classify an email based on the content in the actual body of the email.

Chapter Three: Tasks in Data Mining

The primary objective of data mining is to understand patterns in data. There are two types of functions used in the data mining process depending on the nature of data.

- Descriptive Function
- Classification and Prediction Function

Descriptive Function

The descriptive function helps us to identify the properties of data in a data set. The list of descriptive functions is as follows.

Class and Concept

This consists of data that is related to class and concepts. For instance, consider a business that sells products and services. Class refers to the class of products offered e by the business such as a computer or a printer. Concepts refer to the customers and how they interact with the business. The behavior of the customers would categorize them as big spenders or budget spenders. Since these descriptors tell you about the class and concept of available data, they are called class/concept descriptors. These descriptions can be derived in two ways.

Characterization of Data

In this step, we summarize the data of the class under observation. The class that is under observation is known as the target class.

Discrimination of Data

In this step, we will map the class under observation to an existing class or group.

Frequent Patterns Mining

In a data set, you will often come across recurring data. These are known as frequent patterns of data. Let us go through different types of frequent patterns.

Frequent Sets of Items

Frequent itemsets refer to strings or items that keep reappearing in a data set.

Frequent Subsequence

You will often come across data that will show you that one item is always clubbed with another item. A common example of this is a camera being bought with a memory card.

Frequent Substructure

When you combine itemsets or subsequences with a visual representation such as graphs or trees, it is known as a frequent substructure.

Association Mining

If you were to study data sets concerning retail sales, you would come across patterns that suggest items that are always bought together. This is where association mining helps. It is used to establish an association between products and understand the rules of the association.

A common example of this is when a retailer establishes the relationship that 70% of times when a customer buys milk, they also buy bread with it. And 40% of these times, biscuits are bought along with bread.

Correlation Mining

Correlation mining is going one step ahead of association mining. After the association between items in a data set is established through association mining, correlation mining helps to investigate further relationships between items in the data set to reveal interesting statistics. It also tells us if the associated items in a data set have negative, positive, or zero influence on each other.

Cluster Mining

Data instances that have the same features are known as clusters. Cluster analysis is the phase where data instances exhibiting the same properties are grouped together. This leads to creating multiple clusters where every cluster is unique and different from the other clusters.

Prediction and Classification

The process of building models that would let us know about classes or concepts is known as classification. The classification will further help with the prediction of data classes for which the class labels are unknown. Let us go through a few forms that will tell us more about derived models.

- Decision trees
- Classification rules (If-Then)
- Neural networks
- Mathematical formulae

All the above forms use the following set of functions.

Classification

Classification data sets have object classes that do not have any class labels. Classification helps to predict class labels for such classes.

Prediction

We already know that it is normal for data sets to have missing data. Prediction helps to predict missing data or data that is unavailable for several reasons. Prediction also helps to predict distribution in new data sets by looking at the existing data set. This helps to understand patterns and trends in a data set.

Evolution Analysis

A data model will not always be regular and can change over time. Evolution analysis helps to learn how trends or patterns change over time.

Outlier Analysis

Outliers as already discussed are odd instances of data that do not fit in the remainder of the data set. Outliers are anomalies or irregularities in the data set.

Data Mining Task Primitives

Data mining tasks are executed via a query to extract the required data. The query is fed as an input parameter to the data mining system. Data mining task primitives are used to define the query. Data mining task primitives are as follows.

- How relevant to the task is the data to be mined
- What type of data or knowledge is to be mined
- Historical data to be used to mine and discover new data
- Pattern evaluation thresholds and interestingness of data
- Visual representation of the discovered patterns

How relevant to the task is the data to be mined

This is that part of the database that is relevant to the user. It contains database dimensions and attributes of the data warehouse that would interest a user.

What type of data or knowledge is to be mined

This includes the list of functions that need to be performed. The functions comprise classification, prediction, discrimination, characterization, clustering, association, evolution analysis, outlier analysis, correlation analysis, etc.

Historical data to be used to mine and discover new data

Data can be mined at multiple levels of abstraction given that we have historical data available to us. An example would be hierarchies that empower data mining to be performed at various levels of abstraction.

Pattern evaluation thresholds

Patterns are a result of the knowledge discovery process. These patterns are then evaluated further. Digging deeply through data can reveal interesting facts.

Visual representation of the discovered patterns

After discovering patterns in a data set, representing them visually will help you communicate your findings to senior leadership and other stakeholders of the project. There are various kinds of visualizations available to plot data such as charts, graphs, maps, trees, etc.

Chapter Four: Issues in Data Mining

In this chapter, we will look at the issues that are encountered in the process of data mining. These issues include aspects such as dealing with different data types, methods used for data mining, performance, and user interaction.

Let us cover these in detail.

Issues during User Interaction and Mining Methodology

This section will cover the issues that deal with different types of knowledge mined, mining knowledge at granular levels, domain knowledge, visualization of knowledge, ad hoc mining, etc.

Mining different kinds of knowledge

The pursuit of knowledge is subjective, and it differs from one person to another. Everyone is looking for knowledge and they don't need to be all looking for the same kind of knowledge. Therefore, considering this, we need to ensure that data mining will cover a variety of tasks related to data discovery and analysis that comprise characterization of data, association, classification, discrimination, trend analysis and deviation, similarity analysis, and clustering. There may be a common database for all these tasks, but the techniques used will differ.

Mining knowledge at multiple levels of abstraction

It is necessary to keep the data mining process as interactive as possible since you can never be sure when and how you will find relevant data. If the size of the database is huge, it will be practical to take a sample data set and process it and then apply the findings from the sample set to the rest of the data set. Using interactive techniques in the data mining process, filters can be made available to narrow the search to meet the requirements of the user. This will help attain refined outputs from the data mining activity. The approach toward knowledge mining should ideally be a drill-down, roll-up approach. This means that we need to scan through the available data interactively. An example of this would be how OLAP works with data cubes. By doing this, users can interact with the data at granular levels and get perspective from all angles as and when required.

Background knowledge integration

Knowledge discovery benefits a lot from background knowledge or past data available for the domain under study. Patterns can be discovered and expressed in precise terms and multiple abstraction levels using background knowledge. Integrity constraints and deduction rules are part of database-related domain knowledge that can be used to optimize the process of data mining. Additionally, it also helps you to understand the interestingness in the knowledge patterns.

Ad hoc data mining with Query Languages

SQL or other such relational query languages are used to extract data from a database. High-level query languages are developed by software engineers for advanced data mining tasks. This will enable users to write quick queries for ad hoc data mining assignments by considering relevant data sets for data analysis, knowledge mining of different types, domain knowledge, and conditions and constraints to be applied for patterns. The data mining process can be made flexible and efficient if a query language to work at this level can be developed.

Visual presentation of data mining outputs

After completing the process of data mining or knowledge discovery, you may need to present it in a visual format so that humans can perceive the knowledge and put it to use accordingly. This part is critical if the business requires you to have an interactive data mining system. You can use techniques such as tables, charts, graphs trees, etc. to present knowledge in a visual format.

Managing outliers or incomplete data

We already know that there can be odd data or outliers in a data set. Outliers are unexpected instances of data often referred to as noise, exceptions, or incomplete data. The data mining process can become confusing if outliers are present and can affect the knowledge model. This would mean that the outputs of the data mining process would have poor accuracy for the patterns discovered. Therefore, we need to have cleaning methods in place to filter out the outliers.

Although cleaning methods remove outliers, investigating outliers further can reveal crucial information concerning risk and fraud detection. This process is known as outlier mining.

Pattern Evaluation

A database contains thousands of patterns that can be discovered. Most of these patterns will not be useful to anyone performing data mining on the database as it will not contain any relevant information for the domain under observation. Patterns mined through data mining may not always be interesting and this is still a challenge faced by the data mining process as this can lead to a waste of time and effort. Pattern evaluation will help us measure the interestingness of patterns in a database and help optimize the data mining process for future tasks.

Performance Issues

This section will cover the performance issues faced during the process of data mining. These comprise the scalability and efficiency of data mining algorithms.

Data mining algorithms: efficiency and scalability

It is expected of the data mining algorithm to be efficient and scalable to extract data from huge databases effectively. This means that the runtime of a data mining algorithm in a data mining system should be predictable and acceptable. Algorithms that have polynomial or exponential complexity should be avoided. When it comes to knowledge discovery in databases, efficiency and scalability have always been a challenge for data mining systems. Efficiency and scalability are concerns when it comes to user interaction and mining methodology as well.

Distributed, parallel, and incremental algorithms

The world needs distributed and parallel data mining algorithms. The range of data distribution and the complexity in the data mining methods has given rise to this need. These algorithms have the capacity to split data into various parts and processing them in parallel. The results of individual parts are then merged in the end. The process of data mining can be costly. Therefore, having incremental algorithms that can start the process of data mining, then stop and continue from where they left off can help save a lot of costs. This will help save time, as we won't need to process data from scratch every time. Additionally, incremental algorithms are also beneficial as knowledge is constantly being modified incrementally and previously discovered patterns can be amended too.

Dealing with different data types

Data is as diverse as it can get. In this section, we will talk about issues that arise when dealing with different data types. We will also discuss issues faced while mining data from global systems and heterogeneous databases.

Dealing with complex data types

Databases have various types of data stored in them. Therefore, it is essential to develop data mining systems that are efficient for treating relational databases as they are used in businesses all over the world. At the same time, it is also important to remember that other types of databases comprise multimedia data, spatial data, transaction data, hypertext data, or temporal data. Since we have different data types and the objective of every data mining activity differs from another, it is impractical to think that one data mining system could deal with all of them. Specific data mining systems are required to mine specific types of data. Therefore, it is important to develop data mining systems that can manage different types of data.

Mining information from global systems and heterogeneous databases

Today we have local and wide area networks that connect computers over the Internet. This opens up a gateway to several data sources; these data sources are huge and heterogeneous. These huge data sources over the Internet may or may not be structured, or semi-structured and mining data from them is a big challenge. You cannot use simple queries to mine data from heterogeneous sources of data. Therefore data mining systems need to be developed to improve the process of data exchange over the Internet.

Chapter Five: Terminologies of Data Mining

In this chapter, we will cover the various terminologies in the field of data mining used by data analysts and data scientists. We will cover every term used in the data mining process and discuss each one briefly.

Let us go through each term one by one. We have arranged the terms in alphabetical order so you can locate a term quickly whenever you want.

Accuracy

Accuracy is the most important factor that decides the success rate of a data mining activity. When we talk about accuracy concerning data mining or data in general, it refers to how much percentage of values in the data set is correct. Accuracy is a measure for data models and tells us how well a data set and model fit each other. In short, accuracy is the measure of how efficient and error-free a model is. Accuracy does not take into account information about associated costs. This means that a model that is not very accurate may turn out to be cost-efficient.

Activation Function

The function that transforms infinite sets of data taken from multiple sources into a finite set to insert into a neural node is known as an activation function. It was developed to understand neuron firing better. The activation function would have an original value of 0 and would turn to 1 if it encountered a large input of data. However, it would cause mathematical problems as there is no continuity between 0 to and this led to the development of the logistic function.

Antecedent

We already know that an association exists between two variables in a data set. The variable on the left or the first variable is known as the antecedent. For example, if we look at the association, "When a customer buys one packet of bread, he also buys a bottle of jam 50% of the time", 'buys one packet of bread' is the antecedent.

API

API stands for Application Program Interface. When software engineers develop software, they create a code for API that lets software from outside the code interacts with the code of their software. API also allows third-party software to perform additional tasks on software at times. For example, consider software for data mining, the API for it will allow external users to perform functions such as data extraction, data analysis, model generation, chart creation, etc. The response from the API can then be fed as input into other software as per user requirements.

Association

Association algorithms give you insights about how often events occur together. Again we can look at the same example that we considered before. "When a customer buys one packet of bread, he also buys a bottle of jam 50% of the time" it is the association algorithm that tells you that these events occur together 50% of the time. Such relationships are expressed using a confidence interval.

Backpropagation

A neural network has data with an associated weight. This weight can be calculated using a training method known as backpropagation.

Bias

Some terms constantly occur in a neural network that is known as bias.

Binning

The process of transforming continuous data into discrete data is known as binning. This is done by using a bin identifier that replaces values in a continuous range and each bin is then equal to a range of values. For example, if we have a numeric data set, everything under 15 would be represented by one bin, 16-39 by another bin, 40-55 by another bin, and so on.

Bootstrapping

The original data in a training set is replaced with other data to create more training sets. This may lead to recurring instances of data. In short, bootstrapping assumes the sample data set to be a complete data set. The average of the test sets in bootstrap tests is considered and a final test score is accepted.

CART

CART stands for Classification And Regression Trees. The CART method is used to split independent variables of data into smaller groups. The tinier data sets are then processed using a constant function. The constant function takes small finite values in the form of categorical trees.

For example, True or False, Yes, or No, 1 or 0, etc.

In regression trees, a mean value is added to the small ignite data sets.

Categorical Data

Categorical data indicates the opposite of continuous data and is discrete. Oy can be non-ordered or nominal such as name, age, city, gender, etc. It can also be nominal or ordered such as temperature values that are high, medium, or low.

CHAID

CHAID stands for Chi-squared Automatic Interaction Detector. It is an algorithm that employs the chi-squared statistics to split data into smaller connected sets.

Chi-Squared

Chi-squared is one of the measures used to determine how well a model suits the data. CHAID makes use of chi-squared to fit categorical trees into homogeneous subsets.

Classification

One of the problems in data mining is predicting the category of data. Classification helps to solve this problem by building data models.

Classification tree

A classification tree is a decision tree that puts variable data into classes.

Cleaning or Cleansing

The process that initiates data for data mining is known as cleaning or cleansing. The process is used to eliminate obvious preliminary errors such as incorrect dates or missing data.

Clustering

Clustering is the process of grouping data instances that exhibit similar attributes together. For example, an insurance company would create different groups of customers based on attributes such as income, health history, age, claims history, etc. Clustering helps to categorize instances of data with common attributes in the same group. Every group is then unique compared to another group. This is also commonly referred to as unsupervised learning as the categories are not defined properly most of the time.

Confidence

Consider we have two events A and B. When we have rule B given rule A, it shows the confidence of event B occurring when event A has already occurred. Confidence is measured using percentage values. For example, if the measure were 100%, it would mean that when event A occurs, it is always followed by event B. It is also known as the conditional probability of event B given that event A has happened. If we use confidence along with association, confidence becomes an observational parameter rather than being predictive.

Confusion matrix

A confusion matrix is used to show the actual values of a class as compared to the predicted values of the class. It is an indicator of how good the data model is for prediction, and also tells us where it could have been erroneous.

Consequent

We already know that an association exists between two variables in a data set. The variable on the right or the second variable is known as the consequent. For example, if we look at the association, "When a customer buys one packet of bread, he also buys a bottle of jam 50% of the time", 'buys a bottle of jam' is the antecedent.

Continuous

Real numbers flow continuously and any value can be declared for the continuous data. The value need not necessarily be an integer value. Continuous is the opposite of discrete or categorical data.

Cross-Validation

Cross-validation is a method used to calculate the accuracy of a classification model or a regression model. Data is divided into multiple groups and every group is tested with the model to check if it suits the other groups.

Data

Everything that is available to humans and can be recorded or registered is known as data. It is available in various forms such as numbers, strings, images, videos, etc. The form of data in a database is known as a data type or data format. ,

Data Mining

Data Mining in the field of computer science is the extraction of information from raw data sources that can be used for the benefit of a business or otherwise. Do not compare the term data mining to the general mining process as it can confuse you. When miners extract gold or diamonds from the surface of the earth, the result is gold and diamonds. However, the result of data mining is not data. The objective behind data mining is to extract information from raw data to recognize patterns that will give us insights about the respective data set belonging to a particular domain in life. This is why data mining is often referred to as Knowledge Discovery or Knowledge Extraction as well.

Data Mining Method

The algorithms and procedures used in the process of data mining are known as data mining methods.

DBMS

DBMS stands for Database Management Systems. These are software or systems that are developed for managing data.

Decision Tree

When a set of hierarchical rules is represented in the visual form of a tree resulting in a class or value, it is known as a decision tree.

Deduction

The consequence of processing data using any kind of technique is known as a deduction.

Degree of Fit

The measure of how well a data model is suitable concerning performance for training data is called the degree of fit. One of the most common measures for the degree of fit is R-Square.

Deployment

Once a data model is developed, it is then used for training data. If the model passes the training, it is then accepted. After this, the model is applied to new data for prediction purposes. This indicates that the data model is now ready for deployment in the production environment.

Dimension

When data mining is in progress, every attribute of data is known as a dimension. Data analysts store dimensions either in a flat-file format or in relational databases.

Discrete

If data is not continuous, it is said to be discrete.

Discriminant analysis

Boundaries are used to separate data into categories. These boundaries are determined using a method known as discriminant analysis.

Entropy

Variance statistics are used in data science to measure variability. Another way of measuring variability is entropy. Entropy is also employed by decision trees at times to split data into groups.

Exploratory analysis

Exploratory analysis is a technique used to discover relationships that have not been discovered before. This technique is also used while creating visual representations of data.

External Data

Data that is collected from third-party sources such as books, websites on the Internet, proprietary databases, etc. and excludes data that is present in sources within the organization is known as external data.

Feed-Forward

In a neural network, when the signal is flowing in a single direction i.e. from inputs to outputs, it is known as feed-forward.

Fuzzy Logic

When the data set contains fuzzy sets where the membership can have a probability value between 0 to 1, fuzzy logic is applied. When you have non-fuzzy logic, the output is usually true or false.

However, fuzzy logic also considers the possibility of a 'maybe' between true and false values.

Genetic Algorithms

When you use a combination of input parameters to try and produce optimal outputs, it is called a genetic algorithm. Concepts of natural evolution such as mutation, genetic combination, and natural selection are referred to while using genetic algorithms.

GUI

GUI stands for Graphical User Interface and is the front end that a user interacts with while working with any application. This hides the complex backend of the application from the user and makes tasks comfortable for the user. It is ideally supposed to be very user friendly.

Hidden Nodes

Neural networks have hidden layers within them known as hidden nodes. Unlike input and output nodes, the number of hidden nodes cannot be predetermined. Hidden nodes influence the accuracy of the data model. We need to ensure that a data model has just a sufficient number of hidden nodes, nothing less or more. Today, there are various applications available to scan neural networks for hidden nodes and will choose a model at the end where the hidden nodes do not surpass the data mode.

Independent variable

Variables that are passed as input parameters or predictors in the equation of a data model are known as independent variables. They help predict the dependent or output variable.

Induction

The process used to conclude generalizations from data is known as induction.

Interaction

When there is an association between variables in a data set and changes in one variable influence the other dependent variable, this phenomenon is known as the interaction between the two variables.

Internal Data

Data that is not collected from external sources but from sources that are present within the organization is known as internal data.

K-Nearest Neighbor

K-nearest neighbor is a method used to calculate the distance between an instance of data and its neighbor in a data set. The instance of data then gets assigned to the most common class that is a part of the k-nearest neighbors. The value of k is always an integer.

Kohonen feature map

Patterns in data can be discovered in neural networks using unsupervised learning methods. Such neural networks are known as the Kohonen feature map. Cluster analysis uses the Kohonen feature map on a large scale.

Layer

Neural networks comprise nods that form a group of layers. The layer can be an input layer, hidden layer, or output layer. The number of input or independent nodes and output or dependent nodes is very high with the number of hidden nodes being one or two at the most.

Leaf

The last node of a decision tree that cannot be split further is known as a leaf. A leaf node is where a tree terminates itself.

Learning

Creating new training models with the help of existing models that have been tested in live production environments is called learning.

Left-hand side

We already know that an association exists between two variables in a data set. The variable on the left or the first variable is known as the antecedent. For example, if we look at the association, "When a customer buys one packet of bread, he also buys a bottle of jam 50% of the time", 'buys one packet of bread' is the left-hand side.

Logistic Regression

Linear regression is generally known as a logical regression. It is also called logistic discriminant analysis. Logistic regression models are used to predict binary variables such as 0 or1, true or false, yes or no. For example, a binary value will be assigned to a customer applying for a loan based on factors such as their age, income group, debt, etc.

MARS

MARS stands for Multivariate Adaptive Regression Splines. The generalization of a decision tree is known as MARS.

Maximum Likelihood

Another method used for training or estimation is maximum likelihood. The probability that one specific parameter and its value represent the entire data set that the parameter is part of is known as the maximum likelihood of a parameter.

Mean

The average mathematical value of a set of numeric data is called a mean.

Median

In a continuous data set, the instance of data that tiles exactly in the middle of the data set is known as the median. This means that the number of data instances to the left and right of the median are equal.

Missing Data

There are various reasons such as deletion, incomplete surveys, data loss, etc. due to which data can go missing from a data set. Every data mining process subjectively treats missing data. Missing data is usually ignored, or substituted by mean or median values. Other times, missing data may also reveal interesting facts, and a deeper investigation is pursued.

Mode

The value that keeps recurring the most in a continuous data set is known as the mode. If there is more than one value recurring the same number of times as another value, the data set is called multi-modal.

Model

The result of a data mining function is called a model. There are predictive models and descriptive models. Descriptive models tell us about the underlying process of a data mining approach. For instance, if we look at an association model, we learn consumer behavior from it. A predictive model takes the input of independent variables and gives an output of dependent variables. It helps to predict values that would otherwise be missed.

MPP

MPP stands for Massively Parallel Processing. In short, it is a computer that can control thousands of CPUs parallelly. Every node in an MPP can be a single CPU or a collection of smaller SMP CPUs. A collection of SMP CPUs is also known as an SMP cluster. Every node has a dedicated operating system, disk space, and memory available. Every CPU will work on a different problem parallelly with other CPUs and there is a mechanism set up for enhancing processes too. You need to have specific software to exploit the architecture of this kind.

Neural Network

The human brain is filled with neuron and neural networks is a technique picked up from the human brain to create complex models in the data domain. A neural network is employed to produce dependent outputs by taking in independent inputs. It is used to perform nonlinear transformations by taking linear combinations as input. This is done with the help of the activation function that we discussed earlier. Neural networks use a huge number of parameters to produce an approximate model. Neural networks use present-day data to predict the result in the future. For instance, neural networks can predict who will respond to a mail if it is sent to multiple recipients.

Node

In a decision tree, the point where the decision is made is known as a node. Nodes can also be a point in a decision tree where inputs are taken from other nodes and outputs are produced using an activation function.

Noise

A model is expected to return efficient data mining results. But there will be times when the results will differ from what the model was supposed to predict. This difference is known as noise. When data contains values that were not needed such as errors or data that do not fit the data set, it is called noisy data.

Non-applicable data

Values in a data set that do not make any sense or are invalid are known as non-applicable data. For example, pregnant males, black moon, etc.

Normalize

Consider that we have a numeric data set with us. We take the minimum value in the data set and subtract it from every other value and then divide the result by the range of the data set. The result of this will be a histogram with values between zero and one. This process is known as normalization. Data being input into a neural network or regression model makes use of the normalization process.

OLAP

OLAP stands for Online Analytical Processing. OLAP is a set of tools that can be used to perform multidimensional analysis on a data set.

Optimization Criterion

The optimization of a criterion or a function derived by the difference between estimated data and predicted data is known as the optimization criterion. Maximum likelihood and least-squares are two examples of the optimization criterion.

Outliers

Data that seems odd or does not fit the rest of the data set is known as an outlier. For example, if you are dealing with a numeric data set and then you suddenly come across a non-numeric value, it is an outlier that was not supposed to be a part of the data set. Data that deviates from the standard data in a data set is called an outlier.

Overfitting

A few modeling methods will tend to declare irrelevant data as relevant in the middle of important patterns. This is known as overfitting.

Overlay

Data included in a data set despite not being part of organizational data is known as overlay.

Parallel Processing

When multiple CPUs are harnessed simultaneously to calculate results faster, it is called parallel processing.

Pattern

The point of data mining and analytics is to discover patterns in data. The association between two or more instances of data in a data set is called a pattern. Automated processing is used now to discover complicated patterns hidden inside a data set. A pattern is not the same as a casualty.

Precision

The measure of an estimate's variability in comparison to similar data sets is called precision. If the variation of an estimate is not a lot compared to other data sets, it is called a very precise estimate. Precision cannot be used to measure accuracy. Estimates can always be precise but not accurate, or vice versa. We can call an estimate biased if it is inaccurate but precise. The degree of bias depends on the average distance of the estimate from the actual value.

Prevalence

The measure of how frequently a transaction occurs when a group of items is bought together is known as prevalence. For example, "10% of all the transactions in a retail store included bread and butter bought together".

Pruning

Pruning is the process of discarding all the splits from the lower end of a decision tree. As seen from the name, it is like cutting leaves of an overgrown shrub or tree. The term pruning is also used when the hidden nodes from a neural network are removed to maintain its topology.

Range

The difference between the highest value and the lowest value in a data set is called the range of that data set. You can use the lowest value and highest value together to define the range too. For example, "the range of the data set is from 10 to 20".

RDBMS

RDBMS stands for Relational Database Management System. A system that enables a user to interact with relational databases using software is known as an RDBMS.

Regression Tree

When a decision tree is used to produce continuous variables, it is called a regression tree.

Right-hand side

We already know that an association exists between two variables in a data set. The variable on the right or the second variable is known as the consequent. For example, if we look at the association, "When a customer buys one packet of bread, he also buys a bottle of jam 50% of the time", 'buys a bottle of jam' is the right-hand side.

R-Squared

The method used to evaluate how suitable a model is for training data is called R-squared. The value of R-squared is a value between 0 and 1 where 0 means that the model is not capable of making predictions.

Sampling

When a small set of data is picked from a huge set of data to perform testing to understand the behavior of the entire data set. It is known as sampling.

Sensitivity Analysis

When we change the inputs to a model to see how it affects the outputs, it is known as a sensitivity analysis.

Sequence Discovery

Sequence discovery is very similar to association analysis with the addition of even the time-period being considered for deeper analysis. For example, "50% of people who buy bread buy eggs within the next 3 days".

SMP

SMP stands for Symmetric Multi-Processing. As opposed to the architecture of MMP, in SMP, multiple CPUs share the same resources such as operating systems, memory, and disk space. However, just like MMP, SMP is also capable of working on different parts of a problem simultaneously.

Standardization

This is the process of subtracting the mean or median data value from every value in the data set. The result is then divided by the standard deviation or the data set range. The histogram output for this process is a shape where all values are around zero. Standardization is used when you want to feed inputs into neural networks or regression models.

Support

The measure in percentage of how frequently an association between data instances in a data set occurs together in comparison to the transactions in the data set is known as support. For example, "In 10% of the purchases at a footwear store, both shoes and socks were bought".

Test Data

A data set that excludes the training data set and used to tune a data model is known as test data.

Time Series

Time series refers to the time interval that is considered while analyzing the relationship between items in a data set. Data mining products that work with time series also have time operators such as moving average.

Time Series model

When the past values of a time series are reviewed to predict future values, it is done by employing a time series model.

Topology

The topology for a neural network is defined through the number of layers along with the number of nodes at every layer in the network.

Training Data

The part of a data set that is used to estimate or train a data model is known as a training set.

Transformation

The use of functions such as normalization, standardization, aggregation, etc. to convert data from one for to another is known as transformation.

Validation

Once a model is developed and tested using a training set, they are then tried with different data sets to see if they function in the same way. This process is known as validation.

Variance

Variance is the most commonly used technique for dispersion. In the first steps, the deviation value from the average value is squared.

Then the variability is calculated by averaging the squared deviations.

Visualization

After the data mining process is complete and insights are available from the processed data, they need to be presented visually to the senior leadership and other stakeholders of the project. This process is known as visualization and is usually done with the help of visualization tools to represent data in the form of charts, graphs, maps, etc.

Windowing

Sometimes data will contain time-series data that needs training for a model. This is where the windowing process comes into the picture. The time interval that is invested in training data is known as a window. For example, let us talk about stock market data that is available for fifty weeks every week. A time interval or window can be set for five weeks where the first training case will analyze the behavior over the first five weeks and ultimately predict the result for the sixth week. The data from the sixth week will be used to predict the behavior for the seventh week and so on.

Chapter Six: Data Mining Query Language (DMQL)

We will learn about the Data Mining Query Language in this chapter. We will go through the concepts of the query language, the motivation to develop it, and the syntax used for writing queries that fetch data. Han, Fu, Wang, and others first proposed the data mining query language to be used in integration with the DBMiner system for data mining. The initial proposal comprised a structured data mining query language. Query languages offer support for interactive data mining and ad hoc data mining. Data mining query languages also extend support to data warehouses and databases. The primary objective of data mining query languages is to define data warehouses and data marts.

Let us go through the various syntaxes available for data mining query language based on various scenarios.

General Data Mining Query Language Syntax

The task at hand defines the syntax of data mining query language to be used.

USE database db_name

OR

USE data warehouse dw_name

IN relevance to attribute_or_dimention_list

FROM relation/cube [WHERE condition]

ORDER BY ordered_list

GROUP BY group_list

Data Mining Query Language Syntax Based on the Kind of Knowledge

The syntax in this scenario is classified as follows

- Characterization
- Association
- Discrimination
- Prediction
- Classification

Characterization syntax

The characterization syntax for data mining query language looks like:

MINE characteristics [as pattern_name] analyze {measures}

Analyze operator: Aggregate measures such as sum, count, or count% can be specified here.

Association syntax

The association syntax for data mining query language looks like:

MINE associations [as pattern_name] matching {metapattern}

Discrimination syntax

The discrimination syntax for data mining query language looks like:

MINE comparison [as pattern_name]

FOR {target_class} WHERE {target_condition} versus {contrast_class_i} WHERE {contract_condition_i} analyze {measures}

Prediction syntax

The prediction syntax for data mining query language looks like:

MINE prediction [as pattern_name] analyze {prediction_attribute_or_dimension}

set {attribute_or_dimension_i=value_i}

Classification syntax

The classification syntax for data mining query language looks like:

MINE classification [as pattern_name] analyze {classification_attribute_or_dimension}

Concept Hierarchy Specification Syntax

Concept hierarchy specification uses the following general syntax.

USE hierarchy hierararchy_name FOR attribute_or_dimension

The syntax can be further customized as per

- Schema hierarchies
- Set group hierarchies
- Operation derived hierarchies
- Rule-based hierarchies

Schema hierarchies

The scheme hierarchy syntax for data mining query language looks like:

DEFINE hierarchy time_hierarchy ON date AS [date, month, quarter, year]

Set grouping hierarchies

The set grouping hierarchy syntax for data mining query language looks like:

DEFINE hierarchy age_hierarchy FOR age ON customer AS

level1: {young, middle_aged, senior} < level0: all

level2: {20, …, 39} < level1: young

level3: {40, …, 59} < level1: middle_aged

level4: {60, …, 89} < level1: senior

Operation derived hierarchies

The operation derived hierarchy syntax for data mining query language looks like:

DEFINE hierarchy age_hierarchy FOR age ON customer

AS {age_category(1), …, age_category(5)}

:= cluster(default, age, 5) < all(age)

Rule-based hierarchies

The rule-based hierarchy syntax for data mining query language looks like:

DEFINE hierarchy profit_margin_hierarchy ON item AS

level1: low_profit_margin < level0: all

IF (price-cost)<$50

level1: medium_profit_margin < level0: all

IF (price-cost)>$50 and (price-cost<$250

level1: high_profit_margin < level0: all

Interestingness Measures Specification Syntax

We can use the following syntax to declare the measures and thresholds of interestingness.

WITH <interest_measure_name> threshold = threshold value

Pattern Presentation & Visualization Specification Syntax

This particular syntax comes handy to display the discovered patterns in a required form. It looks like:

DISPLAY as <result_form>

Standardization of Data Mining Query Languages

The following purposes are served by standardizing data mining query language.

- Data mining solutions can be developed using a systematic approach
- It can lead to improvement of the interoperability between data mining systems and the various functions that they use
- It can lead to the promotion of rapid learning and education
- It creates encouragement in the industry and society to adopt data mining systems

The Purpose of Data Mining Query Language

The following purposes are served by data mining query language.

- The data mining query language can be applied to new data to make single or multiple predictions. We can pass individual parameters on in a complete batch.

- The data mining query language can be used to fetch statistical data for the training data.
- Rules and patterns can be extracted for a pattern in a model.
- Calculations such as regression formulae can be extracted to explain patterns.
- We can fetch cases that suit a pattern.
- We can retrieve individual case details for a pattern too. This includes unused data from an analysis.
- New data can be added to a model to retrain it. Cross-prediction can be performed as well.

Chapter Seven: Classification and Prediction in Data Mining

We have been through chapters that introduced us to the concepts of classification and prediction. In this chapter, we will deep dive into classification and prediction and the methods and techniques that these processes use.

There are two types of data analysis that models can use to predict future patterns or trends in data or to describe classes. These are as follows.

- Classification
- Prediction

From the previous chapters, we have established that classification analysis is used when data is categorical, and prediction analysis is used when data is continuous. For instance, we can use classification analysis to categorize the products of a bank such as a loan. Meanwhile, prediction analysis is used to understand the spending pattern of the customer of a bank based on various parameters such as their age, income, social groups, etc.

Let us go through a few more examples to understand classification analysis and prediction analysis. Classification analysis can prove to be beneficial in the following scenarios.

- A banking official from the loan department needs to analyze customer data to understand if it is safe to grant a loan to them or not.
- A marketing executive for a retail company that needs to analyze customer data to see if they will purchase a laptop or not.

If we look at both the examples discussed above, a model classifier is used to assign a categorical label to the loan applicant and the customer. When we look at the loan applicant, the label used will be 'risky or safe', and in the case of the laptop customer, the label will be 'yes or no'.

Similarly, prediction analysis can prove to be beneficial in the following scenarios.

- Consider a sale at Best Buy. The marketing manager at Best Buy wants to know how much a customer will spend on average during the ongoing sale period. The prediction value here is numeric. Given that data, in this case, will be continuous, a model that can predict this or a predictor is the requirement.
- One of the most common methods employed for prediction is regression analysis since it is statistical.

How Classification Works

We will be using the bank loan example to understand how classification works.

Two steps comprise the process of classification.

1. Build a model or a classifier
2. Use the model or the classifier to perform classification

Building a Model or Classifier

This is the first step in the workings of a classifier, known as the learning phase or the learning step. Classifiers are created by developing classification algorithms. A training set is used for the creation of a classifier. The training set comprises database tuples that contain classes and the respective class labels. Every tuple that is part of the training set is known as a category or a class. Tuples also have alternative names such as objects, samples, or data points.

Using the Model or Classifier

This is the second step in a classification where we use the model or classifier that we built in the first step. The test data set is selected and the rules defined in the classifier are used on it. If the accuracy of the classifier is acceptable on the test data set, it can safely be applied to new data.

Issues in Classification and Prediction

The biggest issue in classification and prediction is the preparation of data. The following activities are a part of the data preparation process.

Data Cleaning

As we all know raw data has a lot of missing data or incorrect data known as noise. There are multiple data cleaning techniques available today to solve these problems. Noisy data is cleaned using data smoothing techniques, whereas issues related to missing data are solved by replacing the missing values with the values that have the maximum frequency in the data set.

Relevance Analysis

A data set can have many irrelevant attributes other than the noise that can affect the data mining process. Correlation analysis is used to establish if two or more variables in a data set are related. Irrelevant data is then eliminated from the data set.

Transformation and Reduction of Data

The data is then transformed and reduced to clean data by using the methods mentioned below.

Normalization

Data is transformed using the process of normalization. Data instances from a data set are all scaled such that they all fall in the same range. A few applications if normalization is learning steps, measurements, neural networks, etc.

Generalization

Generalization makes use of concept hierarchies that are used to transform data into higher concepts.

Comparison of Classification and Prediction

Let us use a common set of parameters to draw comparisons between classification and prediction. The following criteria can be used to compare the two.

Accuracy

When we talk about a classifier, accuracy refers to how capable the classifier is. The main task of a classifier is to be accurate at predicting class labels.

In contrast, the accuracy of a predictor depends on how accurately it can predict the attributes of new data.

Speed

A classifier and predictor both make use of the CPU for their functions. Speed will measure how efficient the code of a classifier or a predictor is such that it can use the computational resources as fast as possible and then release them.

Robustness

The ability of a classifier or a predictor to extract data from a noisy data set efficiently is known as robustness.

Scalability

The ability of a classifier or a predictor to efficiently treat data even if it grows in size is known as scalability.

Interpretability

The extent to which a classifier or a predictor can understand data properly is known as interpretability.

Bayesian Classification

Bayesian Classification is a classification algorithm derived from Bayes' theorem. Bayesian classifiers are statistical. Bayesian classifiers are used to predict the probability of membership such as if a tuple is a part of a particular class.

Let us try to understand the Bayes' theorem. The name is derived from its founder Thomas Bayes. There are two types of probabilities.

- Posterior Probability [$P(X \mid Y)$]
- Prior Probability [$P(X)$]

$$P(X \mid Y) = P(Y \mid X)P(X) / P(Y)$$

Where

- X and Y are two events and the probability of Y is not equal to zero $P(Y) \neq 0$
- Given that the event Y is true, $P(X \mid Y)$ gives the conditional probability of event X happening

- Given that the event A is true, P(Y | X) gives the conditional probability of event Y happening
- P(X) and P(Y) gives the probability of the events X or Y happening independent of each other. It is also known as marginal probability

Let us go through a simple example to see how the theorem works.

Say we need to find out a person's probability of having chickenpox if they have had a fever. In this case, 'fever' is considered to be the test and the event is 'chickenpox'.

Let us say chickenpox = X

As per the data available in the hospital, we know that 10 percent of patients in the hospital have chickenpox.

Therefore P(X) = 0.10

Let us say fever = Y

As per the hospital data, we know that 5 percent of the patients have a fever.

Therefore P(Y) = 0.05

Also as per the historical hospital records, we know that of all the patients who had chickenpox, 7 percent had a fever. In other words, the probability of a patient having a fever, given that they have chickenpox is 7 percent.

Therefore P(Y | X) = 0.07

If we put these values into Bayes' theorem,

P(X | Y) = (0.07 * 0.10) / (0.05) = 0.14

Therefore, using this theorem, we have found out that the probability of a patient having chickenpox if they have a fever is 14 percent.

There are two critical terms in the Bayes' Theorem

- Sensitivity
- Specificity

These terms are used to tackle the causes of false positives and false negatives.

Sensitivity

The rate of true positivity is known as sensitivity. It is the measure of positives that have been identified correctly. For example, consider a pregnancy test. Sensitivity here would imply the number of women who took the pregnancy test because they thought they were pregnant. A sensitive test will always be positive.

Specificity

Specificity indicates a true negative test. It is the measure of negatives that are identified correctly. We can again take the pregnancy test as an example. Specificity would imply the number of women who took a negative pregnancy test because they thought they were not pregnant. A specific test will always be a false positive.

An ideal test for sensitivity or specificity will always be 100 percent. However, in real life, there are chances of minor errors, and the Bayes' error rate is used to measure the errors.

Let us use an example to understand this further. We will use the example of a drug test. Let us say that this drug test has a 99 percent result for both sensitivity and specificity. As per the given data, what we know is half a percent of the people are actual drug uses. This means 0.5 percent.

We need to find out if a random person who tested positive on the test is a user or not.

$$P(X \mid Y) = P(Y \mid X)P(X) / P(Y)$$

For the given case, we can rewrite this as

$$P(user \mid +ve) = P(+ve \mid user)P(user) / P(+ve)$$

$$P(user \mid +ve) = P(+ve \mid user)P(user) / [P(+ve \mid user)P(user) + P(+ve \mid non\text{-}user)P(non\text{-}user)]$$

$$P(user \mid +ve) = (0.99 * 0.005) / (0.99 * 0.005 + 0.01 * 0.995)$$

$P(user \mid +ve)$ is approximately equal to 33.2%

This test concludes that the probability of a random person who tested positive on the test is indeed a user is 33 percent. Since this probability is on the lower side, we can safely assume that the user who tested positive on the test may be an occasional user and not a regular user. The test concludes that there are more false positives as compared to true positives.

Due to this, in real-world problems, there is always an understanding reached between sensitivity and specificity. This depends on what is needed in a given scenario. The question asked is if it is okay to miss a positive result or does it make more sense that a negative result is not labeled positively.

Rule-Based Classification

If-then classification

Rules-based classification uses the if-then method rules of classification. The syntax for the if-then rule is as follows.

IF condition THEN conclusion

Let us try to understand this with an example. Let us call this rule R1.

R1: IF age = youth AND job = yes

THEN buys_car = yes

Points to note in the If-Then rule

- The IF part of the rule is known as a precondition or rule antecedent
- The THEN part in the rule is known as the rule consequent
- The IF part of the rule can have one or more conditions in it. If the conditions or tests are more than one, they can be used with a logical AND operator
- The THEN part of the rule is the prediction of the class

We can write the above rule R1 in another way as follows.

R1: (age = youth) ^ (job = yes))(buys car = yes)

If the result of this condition comes true for a tuple, then we can say that the IF condition was met.

Rule Extraction

A rule-based classifier can be built by extracting the If-Then rules from a decision tree. We need to note the following points while extracting rules from a decision tree.

- Every path that starts at the root and ends at the leaf node will have one rule.

- The nodes use a logical AND operator while splitting to form an IF condition known as the antecedent.
- The leaf node then results in the THEN condition forming the consequent.

Rule Pruning

There will be times when you will need to prune a rule. As we have mentioned before pruning refers to the elimination of unwanted leaves from a decision tree. The reasons for pruning are as follows.

- A training set tells us the quality of a rule. The rule performed excellently on a training set but not on a real data set. This is why the rule had to be pruned
- If after pruning a rule R, it results in a better rule than the original rule, it is pruned

One of the most simple and common methods used to prune a rule is FOIL.

For a rule R,

FOIL_Prune = positive - negative / positive + negative

Where

Positive and negative refer to the number of positive and negative tuples in R respectively.

The FOIL_Prune value increases when R is more accurate in the pruning set. Therefore, if the value FOIL_Prune is high, R is pruned.

Chapter Eight: Cluster Analysis in Data Mining

Objects belonging to the same class are known as a cluster. In simple words, objects exhibiting the same attributes are part of the same cluster, and dissimilar objects would be part of another cluster. The process of grouping objects in a class with the same attributes is known as clustering.

We need to take care of the following points about clustering.

- Objects that belong to a cluster are considered to be part of the same group.
- During the process of cluster analysis, objects in a data set are first classified depending on the similarity of their attributes. Then labels are assigned to the groups.
- Clustering has an advantage in comparison to a classification that clustering supports changes. This means that we can discover attributes that differentiate the groups.

Application of Cluster Analysis

Cluster analysis has the following applications.

- Many applications today employ cluster analysis on a large scale such as recognition, image processing, market research, and data analysis.
- Marketing professionals can identify customer groups in their customer base using cluster analysis, which would otherwise be hidden. The customers can be characterized further based on their purchase patterns.
- Cluster analysis is also useful in biology. The taxonomy of plants and animals can be derived and further categorized leading to great insights of their population structure.

- It is also used in the geographic domain where land with similar attributes is classified and stored in a database.
- It also helps in city administration by classifying similar houses in the same group based on their value, location, and type.
- Cluster analysis is also useful for information discovery where internet files can be classified.
- Cluster analysis also helps with outlier analysis and therefore, with the detection of risks and frauds.
- Data distribution can be analyzed via cluster analysis to gain insights about every cluster's attributes.

Need for Clustering in Data Mining

Let us try to learn why clustering is important in data mining.

Scalability

The growing size of data demands clustering algorithms to assure scalability.

Dealing with multiple attributes

There are different types of data in the digital world today such as binary data, categorical data, numerical data, and clustering algorithms are required to sort all these data types.

Cluster Discovery

Clusters are not definite and can be of any shape. We need clustering algorithms that can deal with data of any shape. Algorithms that are capable of dealing only with distance measures in small clusters are not very useful.

High Dimensions

Along with low dimensional data, we also need clusters that can deal with high dimensional data.

Dealing with Noise

We already know that databases contain missing data or noisy data. Some algorithms ignore this data resulting in poor cluster quality.

Interpretability

The result of cluster analysis should be comprehensible, usable, and predictable.

Clustering Methods

The various clustering methods are as follows:

- Partitioning method
- Density-based method
- Hierarchical method
- Grid-based method
- Constraint-based method
- Model-based method

Partitioning method

Consider a database that contains 'n' number of objects and has 'p' number of partitions created for the objects by the partitioning method. The partitions represent a cluster where p<=n. This indicates that the objects are classified into p groups that meet the following requirements.

- Every group has at least one object
- Every object belongs to one group exactly

Also, the following points are worth noting.

- For any given number of partition p, there is an initial partition that is created.
- Objects are then moved from one cluster to another using the technique of iterative relocation until the process complete and every object is part of a cluster.

Density-based method

The notion of density defines the density-based model. The process allows a cluster to keep growing in size until a neighboring cluster exceeds the density threshold. This implies that for each point in a given cluster, a minimum number of points are mandatory for its radius.

Hierarchical method

In the hierarchical method, data objects are decomposed hierarchically. Hierarchical methods are defined by the way hierarchical decomposition takes place. It has two approaches.

Agglomerative Approach

This is known as the bottom-up approach. We study individual objects that are parts of different groups. We then merge objects or groups that are close to each other. This iteration keeps occurring until all objects and groups are merged into a single group post that the process concludes.

Divisive Approach

This is also known as the top-down approach. In this approach, instead of studying a single object, all objects belonging to the same cluster are studied. The process then initiates iterations to split clusters into smaller clusters. This process keeps repeating until all clusters are broken down to a fundamental object.

Both of these processes are rigid. You cannot undo anything after objects have been split or merged.

We can use the following approaches to improve hierarchical clustering.

- We need to observe the links between every object at every stage of hierarchical partitioning.
- We should use a hierarchical agglomerative algorithm to integrate hierarchical agglomeration so that we can group objects into tiny clusters. After this, we can process micro-clusters for macro clustering.

Grid-based method

The method where objects come together and form a grid is known as the grid-based method. It is called a grid-based method because objects are transformed into cells that make them look like a grid. The biggest advantage of this method is the quick processing. It takes very little time to process the data because of the grid structure.

Constraint-based method

We take constraints concerning the users and applications into consideration. We define a constraint as the properties of a cluster or expectations of a user, which may or may not be met. The constraint-based method enables interaction with the cluster. A user or an application defines a constraint.

Model-based method

In this method, we try various models with every cluster until a perfect fit is found for the cluster. The density function is used in this method. Spatial distribution is also employed to show the distribution of data points.

Conclusion

The process of data mining is essential for a business as it helps them to derive insights into existing problems in the system and further helps to improve the system. Organizations can make smarter decisions and solve problems faster by employing data mining techniques. We have established that data mining is a very useful tool for a growing business but we still need to exploit the true potential of data mining. Data mining systems cost a lot and managers can justify the huge costs if these systems can be utilized to increase the revenue of the organization. Senior leaders will take data mining seriously when the costs are justified and accepted.

Organizations should give the same importance to data mining tools as any other tool. An organization should implement the data mining process and then involve everyone so that a feedback loop is created to understand the pros and cons of data mining tools. Feedback processes will help an organization understand if they are lacking somewhere and corrective measures can be taken immediately. For example, if the analysis from a data mining approach is resulting in lowered costs, but at the same time causing a loss in revenue due to a customer leaving over privacy concerns, there is no real growth happening for the organization. With the implementation of a feedback and monitoring process, a problem like this can be fixed immediately to get the organization on the growth track again.

Data mining is just the start. The data mining process does not take decisions itself but gives leaders the insights needed to steer the organization toward success with the correct decisions.

References

https://www.techopedia.com/definition/1181/data-mining

https://www.tutorialspoint.com/data_mining/dm_tasks.htm

https://www.brainkart.com/article/Major-Issues-in-Data-Mining_8312/

http://twocrows.com/data-mining/dm-glossary

https://data-flair.training/blogs/data-mining-query-language/

https://www.tutorialspoint.com/data_mining/dm_classification_prediction.htm

https://www.tutorialspoint.com/data_mining/dm_cluster_analysis.htm

www.ingramcontent.com/pod-product-compliance
Lightning Source LLC
Chambersburg PA
CBHW082118220526
45472CB00009B/2223